San Miguel's Mexican Exteriors

Sandy Baum

Schiffer Publishing Ltd®

4880 Lower Valley Road, Atglen, PA 19310

Other Schiffer Books by Sandy Baum
San Miguel's Mexican Interiors

Library of Congress Control Number: 2008921039

Designed by John P. Cheek
Type set in Novarese Bk BT/Zurich BT
ISBN: 978-0-7643-3004-9
Printed in China

Schiffer Books are available at special discounts for bulk purchases for sales promotions or premiums. Special editions, including personalized covers, corporate imprints, and excerpts can be created in large quantities for special needs. For more information contact the publisher:

Published by Schiffer Publishing Ltd.
4880 Lower Valley Road
Atglen, PA 19310
Phone: (610) 593-1777; Fax: (610) 593-2002
E-mail: Info@schifferbooks.com

For the largest selection of fine reference books on this and related subjects, please visit our web site at
www.schifferbooks.com
We are always looking for people to write books on new and related subjects. If you have an idea for a book please contact us at the above address.

This book may be purchased from the publisher.
Include $3.95 for shipping.
Please try your bookstore first.
You may write for a free catalog.

In Europe, Schiffer books are distributed by
Bushwood Books
6 Marksbury Ave.
Kew Gardens
Surrey TW9 4JF England
Phone: 44 (0) 20 8392-8585; Fax: 44 (0) 20 8392-9876
E-mail: info@bushwoodbooks.co.uk
Website: www.bushwoodbooks.co.uk
Free postage in the U.K., Europe; air mail at cost.

Contents

Acknowledgments ~ *Reconocimientos*

San Miguel de Allende has been my home for the last three years. I was attracted to its laid-back ambience, the cosmopolitan (big city, small town) atmosphere, the architecture, and the quiet magic that seems to permeate the air we breathe. There is a creative community made up of artists of every persuasion including writers, sculptors, painters and photographers just to name a few. This town thrives on the creativity found here.

In putting together this book, my intent was to present a variety of homes, ranging from the Spanish-Colonial era and what some homeowners have done within their 350 year old homes, as well as homes that have been built or remodeled in the last ten years.

This book and its companion, *San Miguel's Mexican Interiors,* would not have been possible without the generosity of the San Miguel homeowners who open their homes every Sunday for the House and Garden tours sponsored by San Miguel's Biblioteca Publica. I apologize, however, since this limited space does not permit the listing of all those generous individuals who allowed me in to photograph their homes.

A special thanks goes to my two editors at Schiffer Publishing, Ltd, Nancy Schiffer and Tina Skinner, for having the patience and foresight to help me see this book to completion.

I hope the readers enjoy the journey into these colorful homes through my camera's eye, thereby witnessing a view that is not available to the average San Miguel visitor.

Introduction ∽ *Introduccion*

San Miguel de Allende, one of the oldest towns in Mexico, had its beginning about the time silver was discovered in Mexico in 1542. San Miguel became famous not for silver mining but as a commercial stopover for the silver-laden wagons coming from the mining towns to the north and west on their way to Queretaro and then continuing on to Mexico City. During the period of silver mining, San Miguel grew into a city of wealth and extravagance; the population swelled and the town was renamed San Miguel el Grande. This was the period when many of the magnificent homes in "El Centro" were built. After years of exploitation, the silver mines petered out and San Miguel went into a slow decline, with the population dwindling to around 5,000 persons. It wasn't until after the war for independence from Spain in 1810 was over, that the town's name was changed to honor its fallen hero, Ignacio Allende.

The streets of San Miguel are a treasure trove of Colonial style architecture, displaying strong Spanish influence with their grand archways and dramatic staircases. The traditional architecture of San Miguel revolves around a central courtyard just inside the entry *zaguan*, adjacent to the street. Outside walls have few, if any openings, and access through the entry into the courtyard from the street is secured by massive wooden doors or iron gates. In the early days, horse-drawn wagons with precious silver cargo entered the courtyards, remaining overnight or longer, protected from outlaws who may have had thoughts regarding this cargo. Today, automobiles have replaced wagons in the courtyards. In homes with access to the roof, a covered terrace is a valuable architectural element, providing additional space for outdoor entertaining, generally with wonderful views of the city.

San Miguel sits at a 6,000 foot elevation, where the air is clear and the sunlight bright with sharp shadows. The days are sunny and warm; the skies are cobalt blue (a brighter blue, many think, than in Santa Fe, New Mexico). You would expect the climate at 6,000 feet to be cold all the time, but not here in the hill country where San Miguel is situated. The average year-round temperature is 75 degrees. Daytime temperatures in summer can reach into the low 90s, but the nights cool down significantly. On winter days, the temperature climbs into the high 70s, while nights sometimes drop down into the mid 30s. Without central heating, some of the winter months can get quite chilly before the sun warms the day.

The traditional San Miguel house has separate fireplaces in many of the rooms which help to alleviate the cold. For some, winter is also a good time to have an electric blanket available for those excessively cold nights. The rainy season usually arrives in late June, and lasts into August. The rain is generally brief with sunshine by the end of the day. A profusion of wild flowers blankets the surrounding countryside in the aftermath of the rainy season.

In the early days, trees were not plentiful and construction lumber was not readily available in the San Miguel area. Until recently, most homes in San Miguel had been constructed using methods dating back to the seventeenth century; only the materials have changed through the years. In the early days, adobe was the material of choice. It was plentiful, easy to make, and the erection process was straightforward. Mix in a little straw with mud and water, pour into a form, let dry in the sun for several days, and presto, you have a building block. The adobe was lighter than the stones found in the area, and because of their shape they were easier to utilize. Also, adobe blocks could be made on site, while rocks had to be quarried and hauled to the building. Adobe, a universal and ancient material, was simple, efficient, economical, and expressive, with excellent color and texture.

Another favorite material, discovered to be plentiful in the local area, was *cantera*, a volcanic stone. In early Mexican history, there was much volcanic activity. *Cantera* was found to have a structural capacity provided by no other material available at that time. Wood was not plentiful in the local area. It was not practical or cost effective to cart construction lumber a great distance from its source. Workmen found that *cantera* had the ability to support great weights, which enabled the construction of second floors through the use of arches, columns, or door and window frames made of this stone. Today, *cantera* is used mostly for embellishments rather than structure. Concrete and rebar are now used for the structural integrity of many-storied residential buildings, with various forms of masonry units such as brick, concrete blocks, adobe, and others as fill-ins between the structural concrete elements.

After the adobe walls were completed, a plaster-like material was used to cover the adobe to protect the walls from the elements. This material had to be replaced frequently as it would flake off, exposing the adobe to the elements which would cause the individual adobe bricks to disintegrate. It didn't take long for the walls to crumble if the protective coat was allowed to go unattended.

The traditional house design incorporated a courtyard surrounded by the house structure. Zero lot lines did not allow walls with windows looking out on adjacent properties. Therefore, all the natural light for the living quarters came from the open courtyard. Later, skylights were introduced in the form of cupolas, rounded dome structures with vertical glass built into the sides, which also brought light from the roof areas reaching dark corners in the rooms below. Today, glass blocks, *translucents,* are set into the roof structure, lighting up the areas below as well.

In the hands of today's young architects, traditional home designs have taken on a whole new direction. Using the same materials as their forefathers, they are creating architectural art, weaving the materials into sensual elegant structures. In Chapter 14, Construction, the results of one young *arquitecto* who introduced steel beams into his residential design can be seen.

CHAPTER 1
Facades ~ *Fachadas*

The street-fronting facades of the homes in San Miguel's "El Centro" were generally only one story, due to the constraints of the building materials available in those early days of the Spanish-Colonial period. The prime building material was adobe bricks, which by themselves, did not have much structural capacity. Enter *cantera* stone, with which the early builders found a material with structural abilities that enabled them to go two and three stories without difficulty, while filling in with adobe. Generally, the facades do not tell the true story of what lies behind. Once inside the front entry door, there may be a two, three and sometimes a four story residence surrounding a central courtyard.

The colors of these two hillside homes are favorite choices in San Miguel de Allende and are made even more attractive with the constantly changing light.

This street scene, though typical and Colonial in character, is one of the reasons many find San Miguel so attractive.

Usually buildings are painted different colors to help tell one from the next and to designate where one property ends and the next begins.

Cantera around windows and doors and wrought iron bars on windows reflects the Spanish-Colonial past. The scuppers canales are also *cantera*.

Here we have another street of colorful houses in the historic centro.

Traditional elements have been used in an untraditional way on this home. Mexican cactus is part of the land-scape.

This is a view of the house from the garden *Jardin*. Irregular shapes and mosaic tiles are featured. The accent egg on the roof tops it all off.

A classic, plain look with local stone used for the driveway and stairway walls.

Classic Colonial *cantera* framed windows and doors are highlighted with a decorative *concha* shell *nicho* with a cross above the door, carved doors, and traditional lights.

This whimsical house really catches your eye.

Another imaginative blue house with *cantera* sculptures.

Lush vegetation fills out this hillside of stair-stepped, mainly earth-toned homes and their many chimneys *chimeneas*.

Local stonework accents soft yellow and earth tones.

Extensive *cantera* of various tones adorns these ancient mesquite doors and creates an impressive facade.

In the foreground is an unfinished brick building with tin roof contrasting with the finished yellow house behind it.

This is a contemporary style bright pink house.

Various styles and elements have been used in this house with rooftop terrace.

Instead of wrought iron bars, these windows have been dressed with balconies.

This building has the traditional high wall topped with *cantera*. A *cantera concha* details the fountain by the wooden doors which are also trimmed with *cantera*.

The balusters between the arches of this old Colonial style building add an interesting detail.

This arches in the corridor and archways as windows of this old Colonial building shows the Spanish influence.

A hillside of simple box style houses. Often the sides of houses are left with the brick exposed and not plastered over or painted because another house will probably be joined to it later.

A multi-level hillside home with a magnificent view of the city.

Interesting angles to fit the home site lend individual style to this home.

This large residence is a contemporary version of an older style.

Opposite page:
The bottom concrete trim of the two wrought iron balcony windows and gargoyle lights are traditional features. Most interesting is the detailed bricked arched window and column.

The walkway is part of a courtyard garden and complements an attractive mission style facade.

Stone, iron work, and earthtone paint complement this multilevel house.

This angled wooden front door is set among a mission style stone façade with *nicho*.

A contemporary building which features a large tree as part of its façade.

This plain façade uses *cantera* around the arched gateway and window. The wrought iron gate allows visibility to the street from the front door.

A contemporary façade with Colonial elements.

Two tones and a painted stripe add interest to this long plain wall.

Brick has been left exposed on the front of this house and used as trim atop the doors and around upper floor windows where the walls have been painted after concrete was applied.

A rusty iron entry door and garage door add interest to this plain façade.

CHAPTER 2
Gates ~ *Verjas*

Many of the residences in the original heart of town had only one door or gate as a means of entering the home from the street. The door or gate was usually of a massive size serving a dual purpose. The door is actually composed of two doors. A smaller one is set into the larger, for homeowners as well as guests, while the larger one containing the smaller was for horse and buggy. Today, however, the horse and buggy have given way to the automobile in most instances and the "garage" has become additional living space within the residence.

These are heavy old mesquite doors with nice black iron straps as trim.

One of San Miguel's famous old carved doors with a brass hand as the door knocker.

A geometric pattern has been used for these wooden garage doors with iron straps and open turned wooden spindles at the top.

These are ornately carved pine entry doors. Wooden doors exposed to the elements require frequent maintenance to preserve the wood and keep them attractive.

This is an ancient mesquite entry door braced with iron straps and cross pieces of wood.

These gates can both be opened for vehicles while people can just use the small door.

An example of a wooden gate with black iron clavos as trim.

A painted metal gate with decorative iron trim.

The carved entry door is sided by windows in the archway.

Here is a wrought iron entry gate to the house and garden.

Framing the old mesquite doors are carved columns from Michoacán topped by a yoke.

Detail of carved door column.

Here is a comical gate which is also a door.

This double iron garage door is also the door for people to enter without a car.

A roll up garage door which has been set into the stone wall.

Handmade folk art gates featuring a face and a Guadalupe.

Double wooden entry doors with *cantera* trim.

This stairway is closed by a wrought iron gate.

These Canal street doors are famous for their ornate carving and beautiful *cantera* trim. In earlier days, they could both be opened for a carriage, or a person could enter from the bottom left door.

Matching wooden garage doors

The garage door is similar to the front door.

This front door is set back in an archway.

This is a mesquite front entry gate.

Plain wooden doors have been ornately trimmed for this entryway.

This formal entry has painted white doors with a weathered look, *cantera* frame and top decoration.

A *cantera* arch frames these iron gates at this front entry.

These wooden doors are framed with *cantera* and have *clavos* for accents.

This is an iron door and gate at the same time.

Iron bars add an interesting geometric pattern on these main entry old painted doors. The high key hole and low mail slot are there to make a statement.

A single wooden carved door with popular motifs is trimmed with carved *cantera*.

These iron doors have been given a rusty finish look which is popular.

Heavy decorated iron garage doors.

Iron straps decorate these simple wooden doors.

This narrow iron door has a Moroccan look, especially with these particular light fixtures on either side.

This iron gate has been covered with wood for more privacy.

The pillars on either side of this iron gate have been painted pink to match the wrought iron.

A peek inside this entry gate shows the tile mural beyond while the cross in the iron gate is also an interesting detail.

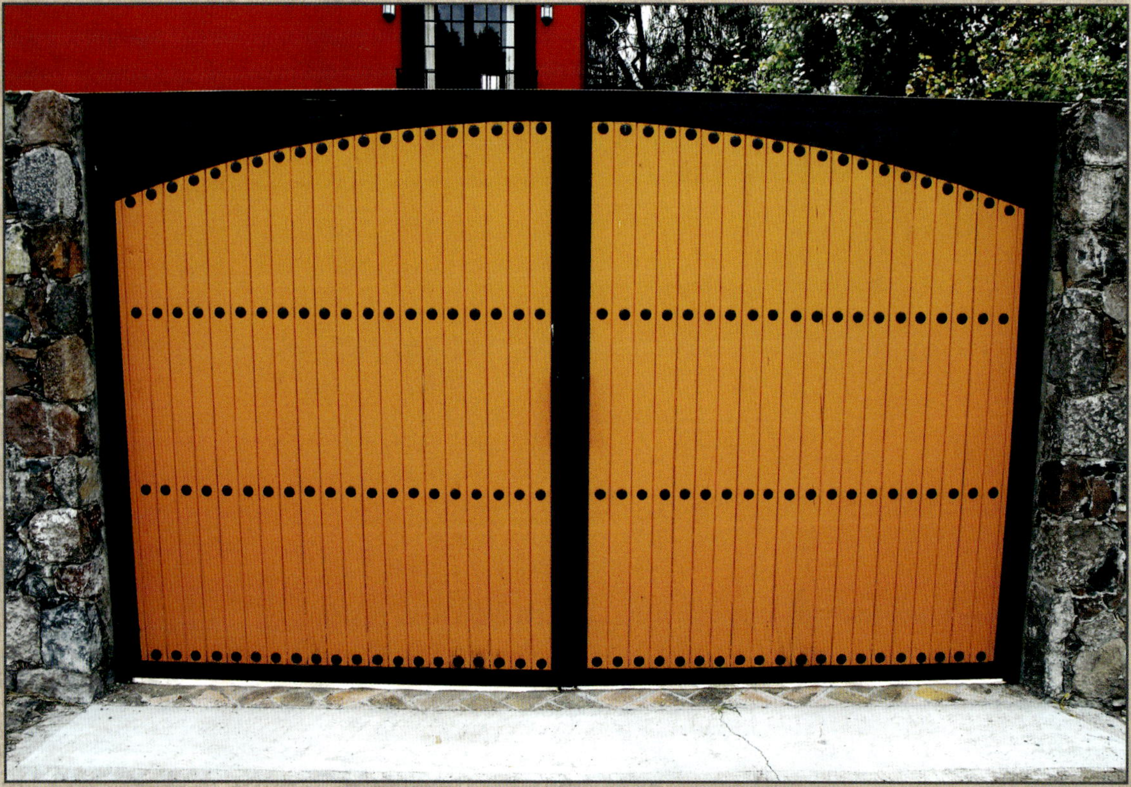

Iron frames the wooden gate and adds the button trim on this gate.

CHAPTER 3

Patios ∽ *Patios*

Outdoor patios here in San Miguel are a great place to enjoy a meal or to entertain. With ideal year-round weather, the patio is a great place for relaxing away from an active home environment or street noises. At any level, patios provide additional light into the living quarters. In homes with access to a roof patio, we find an additional space for outdoor entertaining, generally with a great view of the city.

This walkway has been laid with paver brick in a herringbone pattern and steps up to the upper patio of the same material.

Roof top patios are common in San Miguel and often afford wonderful views. Of course, there are always potted plants.

Just inside the entrance from the street of this home, a small patio with an inviting sitting area welcomes you.

The covered terrace extends the living area of the home.

Another common theme in San Miguel is the central courtyard with access from all the rooms.

This rooftop terrace offers shade and privacy.

The old mesquite shutters frame a mirror on this patio eating area, and large green potted plants complete the scene.

Comfortable upholstered pigskin furniture *equipale* seating picks up color from the yellow walls in this outside patio area. The glass blocks in the tile floor are skylights for the rooms below.

Potted plants line the edge of the wall, as do the tree and plants in the concrete planter box. The comfortable patio seating area is shaded with a large umbrella.

The built-in concrete bench is outfitted with bright blue cushions for comfort and the matching blue cushions on the wrought iron chairs complement an intimate conversation area.

The other side of the previous patio is an eating area with outdoor fireplace for chilly evenings. The blue and white color scheme is carried throughout.

Here, yellow painted walls bring life to the neutral grey furniture complemented by the large, green, potted plants. The *cantera* accent sculpture is the patron saint, San Miguel de Archangel.

A collection of old flower pots *macetas* and *cantera* pieces are displayed on this flagstone patio.

The privacy of a rooftop patio as seen from the street below.

This *sala* is off the master bedroom and becomes an extension of that room, maintaining its intimacy.

Another covered outdoor *sala* off a main room is handsomely decorated and filled with plants.

The fountain cools this covered patio with plenty of room to enjoy meals with guests.

From the lawn, we look back at the *sala* and appreciate the self-contained room with its fourth side open to the yard.

This large *sala* has two fireplaces to accommodate sitting around the table or in the conversation area. The seating is rattan with upholstered cushions. There is even a television, ceiling fan and lights for enjoyment anytime.

Most patios have *saltillo* tile floors as does this one. The old mesquite table is the center of this conversation area with the two handsome carved chairs.

Colorful *talavera* ceramic decorates this patio with the statue standing on an upside down pot on the floor and in the *nicho* painted blue at the back to go with the upholstered seating.

Soft cool, green, lavender, and light blue dress this patio. Even the flowers carry out the color scheme.

On this patio, the table is set and the fountain is turned on for the arriving guests.

Colorful Mexican dinnerware is on the table and the stemware is covered with a decorative netting to keep any bugs or leaves from dropping in. The wrought iron chairs have handsome striped cushions.

Wrought iron table and chairs are common in San Miguel. Often tables are covered with tiles instead of glass topped. *Cantera* birds enjoy the fountain.

This rooftop patio features a view of the surrounding area. Potted plants thrive in the sun.

This covered part of the patio shown above has an entertainment cupboard, sink, and under-the-counter refrigerator. The mirror reflects the view. A pre-Hispanic musical instrument sits on the old bench used as a table in this seating area.

This is a rooftop patio on multi-levels of brick and concrete. A jacaranda tree acts as an umbrella in addition to the green one shown.

This walled patio features beautiful native stone and attractive greenery.

Looking down on this central patio, we can appreciate the two colors of stone and design of the patio floor.

Potted trees and other plants help cool this roof top patio.

The upholstered wicker chairs and matching wooden bench decorate this intimate seating area in this outdoor patio room. The fireplace may rarely be used, but adds to the area.

Just off the main rooms and surrounded by grass, a small patio extends the living area.

This patio extends out from the arcade in the background. Plants surround the water wall.

An open patio is part of this large backyard. The umbrella is usually up for shade.

A large rooftop patio outlined with potted plants. Again, wrought iron furniture with shaded tile tabletop.

Bright pink wrought iron table and chairs accented with turquoise cushions match the color of the glassed dome cupola. The floor of this colorful patio has been painted green to look like grass.

This is a small sun-filled patio with wrought iron furniture.

This rooftop patio is a gardener's delight. Besides, it has privacy and a view.

CHAPTER 4
Gardens ∽ *Jardines*

With year-round temperatures in the mid 70's and an altitude of over 6000 feet, gardens in San Miguel flourish way beyond expectations. Everything blooms from tropical flowering plants and trees found in only the warmest climates to the desert cactus, including, but not limited to bougainvillea, plumeria, agapanthus, schiffeleria, palms, and banana trees. In the hot summers, plants thrive on eastern facing sun but wilt if exposed to the western sun. Many of these plants find shelter under covered patios in colorful *talavera* pots *macetas*.

An iron sculpture in the foreground and *cantera* boat sculpture in the background accent the garden.

Many potted plants outline this rooftop garden.

This garden is dense with large bamboo, ferns and climbing bougainvillea.

Rusty iron mariachis playing various instruments, such as these, are occasionally found as garden sculpture.

Large trees are the center of this stone garden surrounded by various other plants.

Rooftop gardens become lush when filled with potted plants.

Potted plants are often hung on walls in gardens or on rooftops.

Color-filled pots line up along this wall.

Cantera columns support the wood beams filtering the light over this garden and patio.

Stepping stones cross this shallow water garden.

The winding stepping stone path invites strolling through this garden and across the pond.

A brick herringbone pattern walkway winds through this lush green garden.

A mature garden along the driveway with climbing bougainvillea in the background.

This garden is mainly made up of potted plants.

A rosemary plant hangs over this ceramic lady as though she had a head of hair.

Half-round cement and painted planter boxes have been made for larger planting areas than pots afford.

Steps lead up from the patio and through this garden of shaded and sunny areas.

A peek through the trees shows a large green garden.

Dense vegetation surrounds this koi pond in the garden.

The dining room opens out onto this free-form pond and lawn to create a pleasing garden up against the stone wall. Steps at the end lead to guest quarters.

Curved walks, a bridge and a large variety of plants make up this green oasis.

Pots and *cantera* sculptures make up this rooftop garden.

This iron gate opens to the tile-trimmed path through the garden.

A rooftop garden with fountain and flagstone patio.

CHAPTER 5
Fountains ~ *Fuentes*

In architectural circles, the sound water makes as it wends its way down the fountain structure is sometimes called "white or perfume" sound because it masks extraneous noises emanating from outside the immediate area or home, such as voices, ringing telephones or street sounds. Here in San Miguel, fountains come in multi-tiered, free-standing *cantera*, half *cantera* stacked on a wall or a multitude of cascading wall-designed fountains, all making similar sounds and having the same effect...relaxed tranquility.

The fish are also fountains in this pond.

A waterfall drops down into a pond in this garden.

This fountain adds circulating water to the pond while the dog enjoys a drink.

This *cantera* fountain bubbles and dribbles over just a little for effect.

A half-round pond with koi is under the wall fountain.

This bubbling fountain spills over into the pond and runs down a run-off path.

In the lawn area, the bubbling fountain fills the rocky creek bed.

Looking down into the pond, water plants are sunk in pots.

A *cantera* fountain in San Miguel's main garden *Jardin*.

This fountain is at the center of a large colonial courtyard.

A large fountain in a backyard garden.

Some fountains are wall mounted.

A fish becomes a great fountain.

This musician supports a fountain on his head. The overflow fills a pool.

Traditional wall fountains are usually lined with *talavera* tiles and are commonly fronted with potted plants.

A large traditional courtyard fountain is decorated with potted plants.

This is one of 40-plus fountains on the streets of San Miguel. It is more than a hundred years old.

The lion head fountain drips into a collection basin and on into a pool.

This flat star-shaped fountain dribbles over into a blue tiled pool.

Stones have been added for an additional splashing effect in this fountain.

A simple fountain drops water on the round drum and onto the rock filled basin.

A full fountain has been placed in a half-round basin up against the backdrop tiled wall.

Another traditional fountain in the Jardin in San Miguel de Allende.

Talavera tile lines this classic fountain filled with *cantera* birds.

A polished cement wall fountain with the popular quatrefoil window at the top. The bronze frog finishes the scene.

In the old homes and haciendas, this could have been a well, but is now a fountain with a runoff water trough.

CHAPTER 6

Columns ❧ *Columnas*

Materials that make up the columns shown on the following pages are as varied as the *arquitecto* can design them: round, square, *cantera*, brick, concrete, adobe, steel, or sculpted wood.

Still under construction, these columns add height and dimension in the classic style.

Archways support the arcade roof and provide the openness to the garden.

These arches and columns show off the maestro's (master) brick layer's skill.

Another style of brick has been rounded in the arches and columns here. A ledge at the bottom of the columns adds interest and provides a place for potted plants.

Classic *cantera* columns around a central courtyard.

Traditional *cantera* arches and square columns frame this courtyard.

These *cantera* block columns and arches help define the lovely Belles Artes in San Miguel.

Classic *cantera* archways are shown with bulging *cantera* columns.

These column capitals take on a pagoda-like appearance and may be an over-designed element supporting the roof.

These columns give a classy look.

Square brick columns and bricked archways have been used here instead of *cantera*.

These arcade columns are larger at the base, still classic in style.

Mostly columns are *cantera*, but cement columns are often used for a less costly, classic effect.

Here, a detailed square column supports the beam above.

The same square columns support the wood beam covered walkway filtering the bright light.

These columns are carved wood from the state of Michoacán.

Blocks of grey *cantera* form these columns.

These columns go around the outside of the house and alongside the walkway of the garden. They support the wooden beams that keep the sunlight from coming directly in the windows.

CHAPTER 7
Pools ∽ *Albercas*

When you find a pool in the traditional Mexican home here in San Miguel, you find an oasis sparkling in color with the abundance of *talevera* tile so widely found here.

An aerial view of a large compound with pool *alberca* accessible from the main house or *casita*.

This freeform pool has not only a diving board but a Jacuzzi up the stairs. The cool deck around the pool is easy to walk on in the hot sun.

This large backyard pool is surrounded by lawn and a shaded treed area.

This pool affords a view of the surrounding countryside from its expansive deck.

Cantera planters are also a constant source of fresh water into this large backyard pool. A large patio area is off to one side with plenty of room to lounge.

The focal point of this yard is the Jacuzzi, with its sculpture up against the wall, and ground cover edging around the square stones.

An outstanding piece of bronze sculpture watches over the Jacuzzi area.

Water from the mouth of the wall mounted sculpture topped by the classic *concha nicho* accents this shallow pool between the house and yard.

This pool is actually a fish pond for koi. Water shoots upward and the umbrella plants add to the appeal.

Archways and columns complete the far end of this pool's design and large deck.

A large pond with fountain is surrounded with vegetation. Flagstone lines the edge and defines where grass and water meet.

This pool is set in a natural setting of stone and dense plantings.

CHAPTER 8
Cantera ∽ *Cantera*

Cantera, a volcanic stone found to have great structural capacity, was used in the early days to support second and third floor construction through the use of columns, door and window frames and arches made of this stone. Today, we find *cantera* to be used mainly for fountains, columns, both structural as well as non-structural, embellishments as frames around doors and windows, and carved sculptures.

A *cantera* tortoise is a perfect planter for succulents.

This *cantera* figure stands on a wall of the garden.

This *cantera* monkey holds the table top.

A snail keeps an eye on things in the garden.

This carved *cantera* bench up against the building has interesting detail.

This *cantera* bird sits at the edge of the swimming pool. While there is a rock on its back, it could become a glass holder.

A niche has been made for this *cantera* elephant.

This is an old *cantera* fountain in the *Jardin*.

These *cantera* lions with wings are the legs for this tabletop.

A large *cantera* sculpture of three fish has become a fountain in this pool.

This *cantera* fountain is partly submerged in the pool.

This sculpted head stands watch above the street and reminds us of an ancient mythical Greek god.

The couple in the *cantera* boat seem to be paddling along the edge of this garden.

A *cantera* figure adds interest to this garden.

This unusual figure is discreetly hidden in this garden.

This head sculpture almost hides in this garden.

This piece of garden sculpture looks like it escaped from a museum.

Garden sculpture comes in all shapes and sizes.

CHAPTER 9
Windows ~ *Ventanas*

With zero lot lines, buildings adjacent to one another do not have windows on the adjoining walls. As a result, all natural light must come either from windows exposed to the front and back, from open courtyards or patios or from cupolas *cupulas* built on the roofs or translucents (glass blocks) built into the floor or roof structure.

Until recently, all window frames were made of metal. There is no such thing as a "standard" window opening or size. Openings were provided in the construction. The metal shop would send someone out to measure each opening. A frame for each opening would be fabricated and sent out to the site, and eventually glass would be installed after measuring by the glass shop.

The beautiful pink *cantera* framing the window, a pair of antique shutters, and an a partly painted blue ornate wrought iron grill make this window a frequent subject for photographs in San Miguel.

Electrical meters are often enclosed in decorative wrought iron.

The center part of this window opens for ventilation.

A tiled overhang helps keep the rain from coming in the window. Traditional windows open in two parts like this one. Potted flowers fill the window balcony.

Wrought iron bars on windows are as much for the Colonial style as protection. Window sills often become small gardens on their own.

The beautiful rock wall of this building is accented by the classic *cantera* framed windows and wrought iron bars.

While the frame around this window with the overhang and balcony is of a traditional style, the actual window is a different style.

Sometimes *cantera* has been painted over; other times, concrete is used instead of *cantera* and then painted. Since the blue frame on these windows is in sections, it's quite likely it was *cantera* which has been painted. This house definitely stands out with its blue paint job and ornate carved balconies.

Here is a classic quatrefoil shaped window with wrought iron. Remodeling on the inside has made the opening useless, but the traditional design remains exposed.

A round clerestory window looking out through a simple design.

This is a *cantera* framed window reminiscent of Colonial times.

Stained glass is a decorative touch on this arched non-opening window affording softened light.

This small oval window is screened and can be opened for ventilation.

These hand-forged windows are also doors and typical in San Miguel de Allende.

Another window & door with a slightly different arch.

This one-piece oval glass window opens for ventilation.

Elaborate *cantera* frames these windows & doors onto the balcony filled with potted geraniums and other plants.

Quatrefoil windows are usually set in a deep framework like this to help control sunlight.

This oval window offers light and an element of interest to this wall.

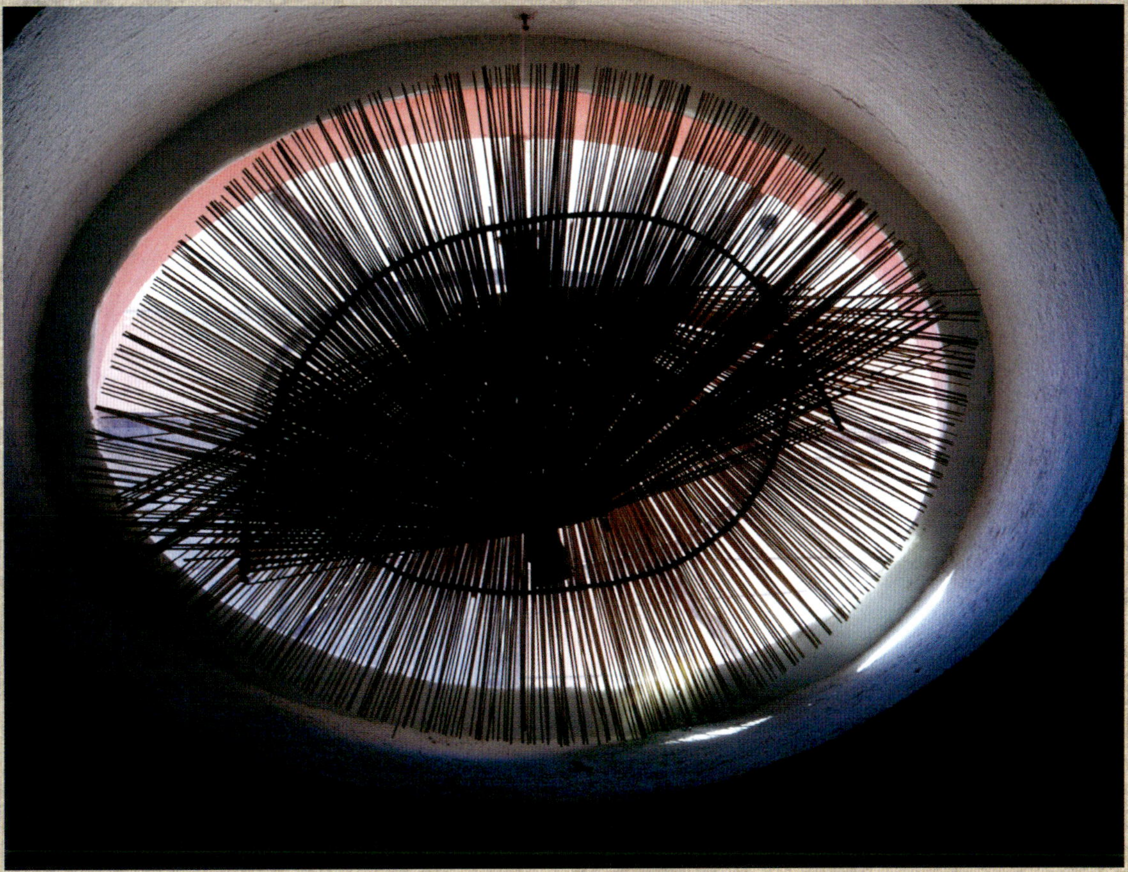

A recessed oval window with a hanging wire sculpture that filters the light.

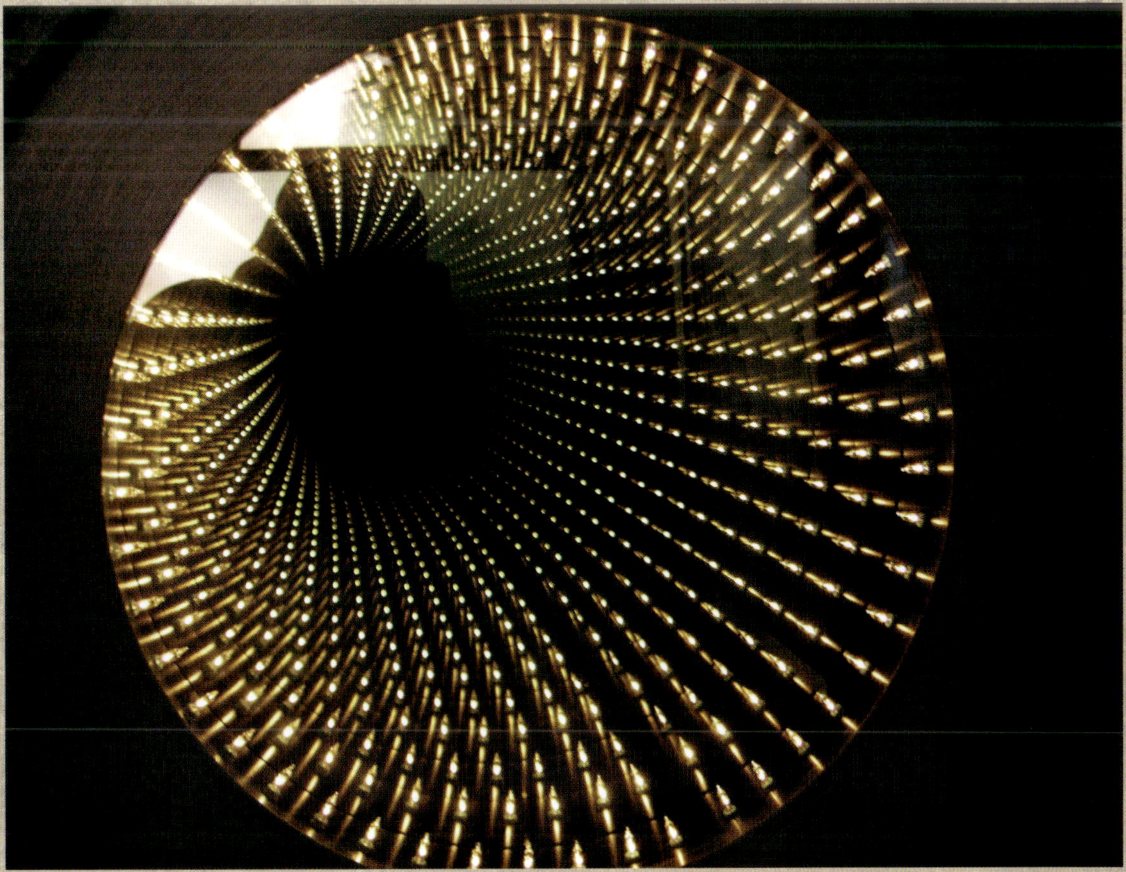

This interesting three-dimensional light display hangs on the wall in this small half-bath under a stairway.

Bars have been added to this oval window on the outside of a house.

This window provides light between two rooms.

This contemporary window in new construction provides outside light to the inside stairwell.

An unusual window on an outside wall.

These radiating iron bars decorate this round window, casting a sun-like shadow.

An iron cross has been added to this quatrefoil opening in this wall.

CHAPTER 10
Walls ~ *Muros*

When you remember that some of the walls you are looking at on the following pages are over 350 years old, you can understand why they look as they do. Suffering from human neglect, Mother Nature has done her best to return some of these walls back to their basic materials, such as dirt, straw and sometimes, small pebbles or large rocks.

Since an adobe wall is the oldest known building block, walls made of adobe bricks suffer the most from neglect and the elements. Long before concrete or brick or rebar, adobe was the only building material the world over.

There are many beautiful stone walls of various colors in San Miguel de Allende. This is a wall that surrounds the grounds at the first church built in San Miguel and features one of the Stations of the Cross.

Mexican mosaic creativity for sure. Leftover tiles and broken tile pieces are used for color and effect with the surrounding block wall painted blue.

Different size bricks and rocks make for an interesting design on this exterior wall.

An adobe-style concrete wall has been accented with special *talavera* tiles. A *cantera* sculpture sits in the *nicho* and a terra cotta wall sconce has been added.

Some of the interest and character of San Miguel are walls like these. They reflect the gone-by years and different attempts at keeping such walls painted.

The plaster has cracked away exposing the adobe brick in this old wall over a doorway.

Brick maestros can be real artists who employ whatever they find around them.

The *cantera* lintel above the doorway is failing but still secured to the wall of the old cemetery by a make-shift wooden frame.

Close-up of the detail of a stone and brick wall.

The plaster-like material covering the rock wall has partly fallen away making an interesting effect and showing the construction work of the original building wall.

CHAPTER 11
Cupolas ~ *Cupulas*

Cupolas *cupulas* are the Mexican answer to skylights for emitting additional light from the roof to otherwise dark corners below. The form and shape of cupolas create a pleasing waterproof structure (generally) with vertical windows allowing light to filter to rooms below, with sunlight bouncing off walls, creating a moving play of sun beams as the day progresses and the sun moves across the sky.

For rain removal from the roofs, in lieu of gutters and downspouts, scuppers *canales* come in all sizes, shapes and lengths. Carrying water from the roof tops, some dribble down on the unwary pedestrian below while others cascade onto the street or parked cars. Many of the home owners have added an extension to carry the water over the sidewalks to the street rather than have the water fall on the sidewalks, a welcome relief for the pedestrians who do not have to detour into the street to avoid the falling water.

This cupola has a sculptured design in the painted concrete with a decorative top. Many windows let in light.

Looking up into the dome of a cupola to show the light from the windows.

This lion is a scupper *canale* which unloads water through its mouth onto the street below.

Maestros try to make each cupola different from the next. This one has been carefully sculpted from concrete and artfully painted.

Another style, more like a tower, this looks like a smaller version of a larger cupola, but is actually a capped chimney flue for the fireplace below.

These cupolas are on San Miguel's most famous church, La Parroquia.

This building has three cupolas lighting various rooms. The fourth structure is a propane tank painted to blend in.

Twin cupolas on a home, plain but functional.

Another plain cupola look-a-like, simply painted, is actually a capped chimney flue for a fire-place below.

This home has different styles of cupolas, serving as light sources as well as chimney flues.

From inside, this cupola with hanging light fixture shows off its brick boveda ceiling.

A simple square cupola, another example of a capped chimney flue.

From this roof top patio and garden, the white cupola adds its own element as the famous La Parroquia looms in the background with its own two cupolas supported on massive domes.

Cupolas are often tiled on top.

Most cupolas are painted to blend in with the surrounding roof structures.

Other cupolas are artistic statements with their own separate coloring.

A beautiful blue-tiled cupola seems to grow out of the bougainvillea.

The maestro had fun with this cupola. It has a Gaudiesque look with all the colorful pieces of tile.

This large square cupola rises to tree-top level and serves as usable living space with a view on the distant landscape.

This traditionally shaped cupola also uses tile above a boveda ceiling and roof structure.

Yet another example of the use of tile for the cupola top. Here, a moon sculpture is atop the stars.

These scuppers *canales* are carved *cantera* fish.

Plain scuppers *canales* extend far away from the building. Some have extension pipes so the water empties onto the street instead of the sidewalk or the pedestrians below.

This older San Miguel building has scuppers *canales* of different animals carved from *cantera*.

Here is an example of a metal extension with a flower surround on a plain *canale*.

Another kind of extension has been added to give a finished look to a more traditional scupper.

A closeup of one of the many scuppers *canales* in the heart of San Miguel.

CHAPTER 12
Wrought Iron ~ *Hierro Forjado*

Wrought iron in the hands of the artisans here is a sight to behold. Working deftly with tools handed down from their ancestors, these artisans create light fixtures, candle holders, gates, fencing, and window security just to name a few of the items that make their way from raw material to a finished product, many 'one-of-a-kind', never to be repeated. Provide these individual artisans with a dimensioned sketch and come back in a week for the finished product.

San Miguel iron workers are famous for their designs. This driveway and entry gate is examples of the beautiful ornate work they do.

Different elements of design have been incorporated in this ornate driveway gate. It has been painted to prevent rust.

This tall gate is both creative and secure with its closely spaced bars and sharp tops.

Newly-made iron lights are in place. The light bulbs and glass will be added later.

A closeup of a classic shaped outside light.

This ironwork goes nicely with the stone and tile-topped gate houses.

An iron and glass entry door.

This iron and glass entry door is inside the courtyard.

From inside the house, through the inner courtyard, the outside doors to the street are seen.

Some wrought iron doors are geometric in design and evoke thoughts of a distant place and another time.

Secure iron work, functional and attractive as well.

An ornate, blue-painted iron gate to the parking area of this house.

Closeup of a creative ironwork design, part of the second floor railing.

Close-up of an iron gate detail.

A decorative iron fence around a monument says, "No Entry."

Closeup of the monument's iron fence.

A very detailed iron gate.

Close-up detail of the previous gate photo.

This black iron gate closes off the parking area and house.

Another parking area wrought iron gate. These open car ports are often still called garages in San Miguel.

These wrought iron gates are fanciful.

A secure wrought iron gate to which chicken wire has been added to keep small animals in or out.

Open iron work shows off the garden inside.

This iron gate has an automatic opener.

This wrought iron entry gate allows those passing by to appreciate the old painted doors.

This is another view of what is often appreciated on the inside of entry gates.

CHAPTER 13
Street Graphics ~ *Calle Graficos*

Marshall McLuhan, a famous advertising guru, once said, "The medium is the message," words that are certainly true here in San Miguel, a walking city and a shopper's paradise. With our narrow streets, street graphics *calle graficos* are most important as any shopper knows, for without them, it would be like walking through a maze where everything looked the same. With street graphics, there is almost always immediate recognition.

Signs on the stores *tiendas* vary in size, usually matching the size of the establishment. Because some of the streets are so narrow, some of the signs are not visible until you are directly in front of them.

This is not a Mexican motif, but a Mexican's version of a wall mural.

The medium is the message.

Old signs, newer signs, and directional arrows.

Some house addresses are hard to find, but no one could miss this house number.

House signs are often the family name, but some would rather make a comment, as on this *talavera* plaque.

A famous store in San Miguel with its hand-painted wall sign.

Another hand-painted sign, clear and nicely decorated.

Still in keeping with the local sign ordinance, this jewelry store has a clear cover over its sign.

An example of an unobtrusive sign.

This sign consists of brass letters on wood, mounted on a yellow wall.

This signage conforms to the chain's requirements, but also fits San Miguel's signage ordinance.

Hand-painted talavera tiles make up this sign.

A temporary poster announcing an up-coming event, secured over other temporary posters on top of other temporary posters.

A nicely done hand-painted sign announcing this street address.

Another hand-painted sign in front of this art gallery.

This sign is raised concrete and then painted on the building.

A coffee house sign with coffee beans on the busy background.

This painted sign has been hung on the building.

Painted signs on buildings are easy to paint over and replace if a store moves away or goes out of business.

This classy Italian restaurant has a sign of individual letters and its logo which stand out on the building.

CHAPTER 14
Construction ~ *Construccion*

The construction methods are evolving in San Miguel, but basic building construction uses the same methods as in the last 200 years, either concrete and brick or brick and concrete with a stucco-like material troweled on for a more finished look. Wood was formerly used only on interiors to support the floor or roof above. Today, with construction wood more plentiful, we are finding more and more used on the exterior roof-top patio roofs. And, too, a wood patio structure above the house roof in lieu of concrete and brick does not require the same building permit here in San Miguel.

Because wood construction here doesn't receive the same attention as back in the States, house carpenters are few in number. As a result when a local builder was contracted to do a wood patio roof, he hired cabinet makers to erect the wood structure. The end result was truly a sight to behold and is included in this chapter.

Brick has been used to make the columns and trim around doorways in this house. The brick structure itself has been plastered and painted. The neighbor has left an outside wall unfinished as is commonly done. A stone wall is often used. Roofs are beams and tile.

Columns support wooden beams to filter the light along this walk.

A large beam is embedded in the stone wall and supports the cross beams in this construction.

A detailed look at the typical post and beam construction with rafters and stringers supporting the tile roof.

Support beams rest on columns, and rafters with tubular metal stringers provide support for the roof tile.

Detail look at the cut ends of the rafters extending beyond the square beam.

Typical wood post and beam construction. Metal collars or saddles were hand-made since no standard brackets were available.

Here, logs have been used for support and cross beams.

The notched beams and tubular metal stringers support these roof tiles.

Close-up of the hand-hewn log and tile roof.

Local stone has been used for the walls and foundation of this house. Concrete and rebar make up the structural components while brick is used as a fill-in. This is an example of today's typical method of constructing houses.

Typical house construction with concrete columns and beams with non-structural brick fill-ins. Available today, are pre-stressed concrete beams that span up to thirty-two feet. This view is the entry stair to the upper level.

The outside brick walls are up, and the orange electrical casings dangle from this structure. The brick and wooden beam ceiling are in place, and a steel beam helps support the floor above.

Outside steel beams add support to this structure.

CHAPTER 15
Colors ~ *Colours*

San Miguel had been a place lacking in colorful expression and, only recently, has blossomed forth in vibrant, bright colors. Along with its brilliant natural light and a cobalt blue sky matched no where else, San Miguel has emerged as if from a cocoon with its cornucopia of rainbow colors splashed on walls and rooftops. Mexicans have even painted their interior walls with the brightest colors as well. The use of bright colors was introduced by the famous Mexican *arquitecto*, Luis Barragan, and today has been carried forth by young aspiring Mexican architects. Color definitely reflects the Mexican spirit found here. Color is everywhere.

The paint colors used in this chapter are available from a variety of paint stores here in San Miguel. You only need to show a sample of the color you want and they will match it or come very close. Technology is not a stranger in San Miguel.

Red and yellow are favorite Mexican colors. In between, variations like orange, terra cotta and rust catch the sunlight and accent the bright blue skies.

The rusty brown iron doors go well with the soft yellow painted house.

Blue stands out more and some prefer this to blending in.

A dark terra cotta painted wall with a turquoise-painted window frame creates an interesting accent.

Turquoise and soft yellow have been used with the terra cotta accent.

A round *cantera* framed window is surrounded by a bright Mexican Red painted wall.

A lighter, softer terra cotta paint color.

Mustard walls with pink *cantera* frame the door and window.

A two-tone terra cotta painted wall brightens this streetscape.

Glossary ~ *Glosario*

Agua- Water
A la derecha- To the right
Alberca- Pool
Amigo- Friend
Arboles- Trees
Arcada- Arcade
Armario- Cabinet
Arquitecto- Architect
Artes- Arts
Azul- Blue
Azulejo- Tile

Balaustrada- Balustrade
Banco- Bench
Bandidos- Bandits
Ban□o- Bathroom
Boveda- Vault
Brasero- Brazier

Canalon- Gutter
Cantera- Volcanic stone
Cantina- Bar
Cartas- Letters
Casa- House
Cascada- Waterfall
Casita- Small house
Chimenea- Fireplace
Clavo- Nail
Cobalto- Colbalt
Cochera- Garage
Cocina- Kitchen
Columna- Column
Comal- Earthen pot
Comedor- Dining room
Comoda- Chest of drawers
Cornisa- Cornice
Corredor- Corridor
Cristo- Christ
Cupula- Cupola or dome

Entrada- Entryway
Equipale- Pigskin furniture
Escalera- Stairway

Fabrica- Fabricate
Fachada- Facade
Flores- Flowers
Fuenta- Fountain

Hierro- Iron
Hombre- Man

Iglesia- Church
Iluminacion- Lighting

Jardin- Garden
Jarrones- Large jars

Katrina- Female skeleton

Laja- Flat rock
Llamador- Door

Maceta- Flowerpot
Maestro- Master craftsman
Mariachi- Mariachi street band
Mascara- Mask
Mensula- Bracket
Moldura- Molding

Nicho- Niche

Ojo- Eye

Petates- Reed mats
Petatillo- A thin brick
Pilar- Pillar
Portal- Foyer
Portico- Covered porch at entry
Porton- Large door
Postigo- Small door usually inside another door
Puerta- Door

Recamara- Bedroom
Reja- Iron grating or railing
Retablo- Religious painting

Sala- Living room
Santo- Saint
Silla- Chair
Sillar- A masonry unit a little larger than a 8″x 8″x16″ concrete block
Sillon- Couch

Tablero- Panel of tiles
Talavera- Hand-painted- twice-fired- tin-glazed earthenware

Troje- Wooden house

Vestibulo- Hall or public lobby
Viga- Beam or girder

Zaguan- Passage from street to inner courtyard
Zocalo- Baseboard

Resources ~ *Recursos*

LIFESTYLE, FOOD & TABLETOP

Bonanza
Mesones 43
152 1260
A complete in-town supermarket with hard-to-find imported ítems.

De Talavera
Puebla No. 60 esq.
Tamaulipas
Delores Hidalgo, Gto.
(418) 182 0749
An extensive line of Talavera dinnerware.

La Buena Vida
Hernandez Macias 72
152 2211
Bakery & Cafe
Natural whole grain breads, French baquettes and unique pastries.

La Europea
Canal 13
152 2003
An extensive selection of wines and spirits.

Petitfour
Mesones 99
154 4010
Pastry shop, bar and café. Homemade chocolates, cakes, pies, and French pastries.

FURNITURE

Arden Casa de Muebles
Libr. Celaya a Delores 26
154 8010
Furniture and home decor accessories.

Camila
Sollano 30
152 2697
Antique furniture, etched glass, custom made inens, & table cloths.

Casa Canal
Canal 3
152 0479
Hand carved Furniture.

Casa del Inquisidor
Aldama 1
154 6868
Household accessories and an extensive hardware selection.

Casa Marie Luisa
Ancha Sn Antonio 26
152 2983
Furniture and home decor accessories.

Coba Art Décor
Juarez 7
154 7516
Interior design, accessories and fine furniture from India.

Colección Cuatro Vientos
Sollano 31
154 9132
Furniture and home decor accessories.

C. Dewayne Youts
Fabrica la Aurora
152 5481
Manufacturer of wood and iron furniture, 17th century reproductions, custom kitchens and accessories.

El Progresso
Road to Delores Hidalgo
(418) 120 3048
Hand-crafted furniture.

Evos
Hernandez Macias 55
152 0813

Classic San Miguel style home furnishings, Spanish Colonial furniture, imported sofas, upholstered furniture & fabrics, and oriental rugs.

Finca
Fabrica la Aurora
154 8323
Furniture, accessories and interiors.

Hacienda la Diligencia
Hernandez Macias 118
152 1626
Custom furniture made to your design and specifications.

Manuel Padron
Santa Clara
Progresso2004@prodigy.net.mx
Hand-crafted furniture.

Marcia Bland Brown
Hacienda Calderón
044 415 153 3176
Furniture design & manufacturing, antiques, interior & architectural design and restoration.

Namuh Collection
Camino Alcocer Km 2.2
154 8080
Indoor/outdoor furniture and accessories from Asia.

SHOPS

Antigua Casa Canela
Umaran 20
152 1880
Antiques, Colonial art and home décor accessories.

Artes de México
Calzada de la Aurora 47
152 0764
Mexican arts and crafts, tin ornaments, Colonial furniture and folk art.

ArtesMéxico
Zacateros 81A
154 8531
Quality hand-wrought opper.

Azulejos Talavera Cortes S.A. de C.V.
Aldama No. 18
Delores Hidalgo, C.I.N., GTO., México
(418) 182 1168
Finest glazed Talavera tiles for floor finishing as well as an infinite range of accessories.

Buenas Noches
Fabrica la Aurora
154 9624
Fine bed and bath furnishings.

Cantadora
Fabrica la Aurora
154 8302
Cantera, fireplaces, columns, door frames and decorative accessories.

Carrillo Vertix Hermanos
Puebla No. 54
Delores Hidalgo, C.I.N., GTO., México
(418) 182 0122
Talavera tiles, traditional and Barcelona, murals and accessories.

Casa Coloniales
Canal 36
152 0286
Furniture, upholstery, fabrics, trim, pillows, spreads, curtains, rugs, chandeliers, sconces, stone ornaments and gifts.

Casa Roberto
Libr a Queretaro 35
152 8620
Lighting, ceiling fans, water filters, purifiers, radiant heaters and fireplace accessories.

Galería Tesoro
Recreo 8B
154 5595
Folk art and home decor accessories.

Icpalli
Correo 43
152 1236
Fabric for interior design, window treatment, furniture and home accessories.

Icons
Pila Seca 3
152 5762
Traditional Byzantine Images.

Ilunina San Miguel
Calzada de la Luz 51
154 7643
Commercial & residential lighting, chandeliers, lamps and sconces.

Lan Art
Ancha de San Antonio
152 1566
Rugs, bedspreads, pillows and household accessories.

La Victoriana
Hernandez Macias 72
152 6903
Botanical beauty products, herbal and homeoathic remedies, flower essence and aromatherapy.

La Zandunga
Hernandez Macias 129
152 4608
Fine Mexican rugs.

Mitu Atelier
Sollano 32
044 415 117 9431
Home accessories, custom furniture and antiques.

Productos Herco, S.A.
Relox #12
152 1434
A large selection of faucets, sinks, bath tubs in various materials including copper and marble, decorative hardware and kitchen accessories.

Sisal
Fabrica la Aurora
154 8944
Home decor and interior design.

Sollano 16
Sollano 16
154 8872
Lifestyle & home décor and accessories.

Talavera Vázquez
Puebla No. 56
Delores Hidalgo, C.I.N., GTO., México
(418) 182 2914
Talavera tiles, flowerpots, murals and earthenware.

Zocalo
Hernandez Macias 110
152 0663
Fine Mexican folk art and furniture and hand-blown glassware.

BOOKSELLERS

Casa de Papel
Mesones 57
154 5187
Greeting cards, journals, photo albums, candles, guide books, road maps, Mexican cook books, prints, posters and CDs.

El Colibi
Sollano30
152 0751
Spanish language books, art books and artists' materials.

El Pato
M Ledesma 19
152 1543
Art supplies, design & accessories.

Lagundi
Umaran 17
152 0830
Art supplies, frames and framing, posters, original prints, books and magazines.

La Tienda Bibliotec Publica
Insurgentes 25
1522 0293
English language books, Mexican history, arts and crafts

Libros el Tecolote
Jesús 11
152 7395
English language books, Mexican history, literature, art & design books.

SERVICES

Fortuna
Pila Seca 3
152 7782
Specialists in conservation & preservation of fine art, photographs, textiles and memorabilia.

WEARABLE ART

Barbara Porter
Zacateros 47
152 7463
Fashion designs for men & women.

Black & White
Loreto 20
154 4493
Traveling clothes, alpaca sweaters and accessories.

Caracol Collection
Cuadrante 30
152 1617
Fine and applied art, furniture, arte copper and ceramics.

Christofas
Cuadrante 2
154 9392
Unique designer jewelry, sculpture, décor art, mobiles and gemstones.

Creación Marcela Andre
Sn Francisco 7
154 9868
Original art, jewelry and decorations.

Diva
Hernandez Macias 72
152 4980
Jewelry, accessories and creative quality clothes in European linens.

Girasol
Sn Francisco 72
152 2734
Mexican casuals

Goldie Designs
Zacateros 19
154 7521
Classic clothing, elegant jewelry and custom accessories

Nuevo México
Aparicio 1
152 4510
Navajo style crafts

7th Heaven
Sollano 13
154 4677
Unique jewelry, art, gifts and clothes

GALLERIES

Atenea Gallery
Jesús 2
152 0785
Paintings, sculpture, graphics, jewelry and art objects.

Casa Diana Art Gallery
Recreo 48
152 0885
An exclusive art gallery featuring paintings and sculpture.

Galeria Aotonileo
185 2225
Exceptional Mexican folk art, historic photographs, vintage textiles

Galería Aspen
Mesones 74
154 4441
Investment art.

Galería Izamal
Mesones 80
154 5409
Paintings and jewelry design by local artists in this cooperative gallery.

Galería Mariposa
Recreo 36
152 4488
Specializing in one-of-a-kind pieces by the great masters of Mexican folk Art.

Galería Pérgola
Instituto Allende
154 5595
Mexican fine art

Galería San Miguel
Plaza Principle 14
152 0454
Contemporary works of art.

Generator Gallery
Fabrica la Aurora
154 9588

INFORMATION

Atencion
Insurgentes 25
152 3770

Promoción Mexican culture (PMC)
Hidalgo 18
152 0121

Tourist Information
Plaza Principal #10
120 4520

Bibliography ⁓ *Bibliografia*

Barragan, The Complete Works. New York: Princeton Architectural Press, 1996.

de Haro, Fernando and Omar Fuentes. *Arquitectos Mexicanos, Una Visipn Contemporanea.* México D.F.: Arquitectos Mexicanos Editores S.A. de C.V., 2004.

------. *Mexican Interiors*: *Style & Personality*. México D.F.: Arquitectos Mexicanos Editores S.A. de C.V., 2003.

Levick, Melba and Gina Hyams. *Mexicasa, The Enchanting Inns and Haciendas of Mexico*. San Francisco: Chronicle Books, 2001.

Levick, Melba, Tony Cohan and Masako Takahashi. *Mexicolor: The Spirit of Mexican Design.* San Francisco: Chronicle Books, 1998.

Luscombe-Whyte, Mark and Dominic Bradbury. *Mexico Architecture, Interiors & Design.* New York: Harper Collins Publishers, 2004.

Stoeltie, Barbara and Rene Stoeltie. *Living in Mexico: Vivre au Mexique:* Cologne: Taschen, 2004.

Streeter-Porter, Tim. *Casa Mexicana: The Architecture, Design and Style of Mexico*. New York: Stewart, Tabori & Chang, 1994.

Villela, Khristaan, Ellen Bradbury and Logan Wagner. *Contemporary Mexican Design and Architecture.* Layton, Utah: GibbsSmith, Publisher, 2002.

Yampolsky, Mariana and Chloe Sayer. *The Traditional Architecture of Mexico.* New York: Thames and Hudson, 1993.

Ypma, Herbert. *Mexican Contemporary.* New York: Stewart, Tabori & Chang, 1997.